ABSOLUTE BEGINNERS
Guitar

AMSCO PUBLICATIONS

London/New York/Paris/Sydney/Copenhagen/Berlin/Madrid/Hong Kong/Tokyo

Exclusive Distributors:
Music Sales Corporation
180 Madison Avenue, 24th Floor,
New York NY 10016, USA.

Music Sales Limited 14-15
Berners Street, London
W1T 3LJ, UK.

Music Sales Pty Limited
Units 3-4, 17 Willfox Street, Condell Park,
NSW 2200, Australia.

Order No. AM973709
ISBN 978-0-8256-1922-9
This book © Copyright 2014 by Wise Publications,
A Division of Music Sales Corporation, New York.

www.musicsales.com

Written by Arthur Dick.
Photographs by George Taylor.
Book design by Chloë Alexander.
Model: Jim Benham.

Printed in Great Britain.

Contents

Introduction

Welcome to *Absolute Beginners for Guitar.*
The guitar remains one of the world's most popular instruments – this book will guide you from the very first time you take your guitar out of its case, to playing your first song.

Easy-to-follow instructions
will guide you through

• how to look after your guitar,
• how to tune it
• how to look after your instrument
• learning your first chords
• playing your first song

Play along with the backing track as you learn – the specially recorded audio will let you hear how the music should sound – then try playing the part yourself.

Practice regularly and often. Twenty minutes every day is far better than two hours on the weekend with nothing in between. Not only are you training your brain to understand how to play the guitar, you are also teaching your muscles to memorize certain repeated actions.

In the back of this book you will find a section introducing some of the music available for guitar. It will guide you to exactly the kind of music you want to play – whether it's a comprehensive tutorial series, rock licks, jazz and blues, easy-to-play tunes or "off the record" transcriptions, there's something there for all interests.

There are two main types of guitar.

The acoustic guitar has a hollow body which allows the sound of the vibrating string to be transmitted through the round soundhole.

Most electric guitars have solid bodies, so the string vibration is not particularly audible – that's why they have to be plugged into an amplifier.

Although the sound and character of acoustic and electric guitars are quite different, the principle workings are the same.

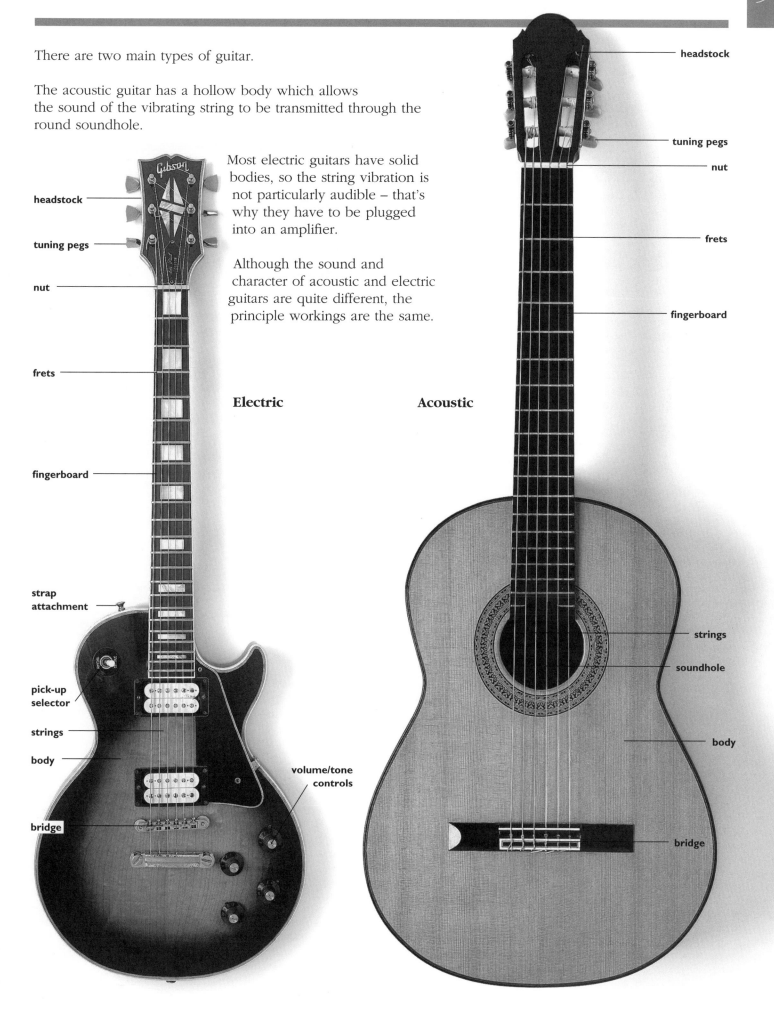

Electric

headstock

tuning pegs

nut

frets

fingerboard

strap attachment

pick-up selector

strings

body

bridge

volume/tone controls

Acoustic

headstock

tuning pegs

nut

frets

fingerboard

strings

soundhole

body

bridge

Know your guitar

The headstock (at the end of the fretboard) has six tuning pegs, either three each side or all six in a row.

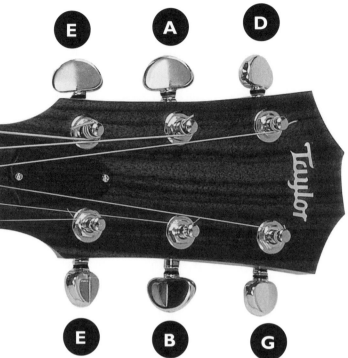

The tuning pegs, or machine heads, consist of a metal capstan and a cog to tension the string.

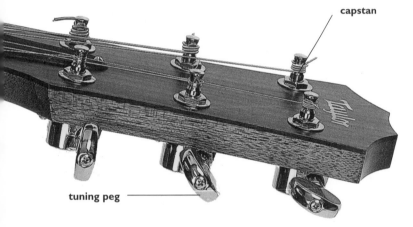

The strings traverse the fretboard (usually rosewood or maple) which may have plastic or tortoiseshell inlays to help you see where you are on the neck.

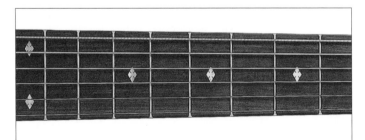

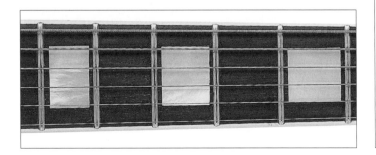

The strings are kept in place by the nut as they leave the headstock.

There are dots on the side of the neck at given fret positions as well.

The strings are attached to the body at the bridge, which comes in all shapes and sizes depending on the guitar, but in all cases acts to alter the harmonics and string height.

The bridge on an acoustic guitar is normally fixed and is therefore not adjustable, but on electrics a wide range of string adjustments can usually be made.

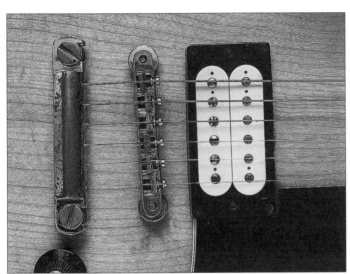

▲ **Bridge – electric guitar**

▲ **Bridge – acoustic guitar**

Below the strings and bridge most electric guitars have controls for volume and tone.

The pick-up selector on the Les Paul type guitar is positioned above the strings; on the Fender Stratocaster type it can be found below.

Most electric guitars come with a strap attachment.

Tip

When not being played, try to keep your guitar in its case, away from heat and direct sunlight, where it can't be knocked over. Avoid exposing the instrument to extremes of temperature.

Strings and things

There is nothing quite like the tone of new strings on your guitar, but that sound will soon fade. Strings are made from alloy and tarnish easily, thus losing tone. To extend their life always wipe down the instrument at the end of each playing session, taking special care with the strings. A clean dry linen or silk cloth wiped over the strings will remove dirt and moisture.

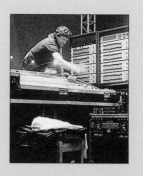

Professional guitarists have a 'guitar tech' or 'roadie' to change strings for them – they're on hand throughout a gig in case a string breaks during the performance. It's their job to make sure all the guitars are in tune and set up in exactly the right way for that guitarist.

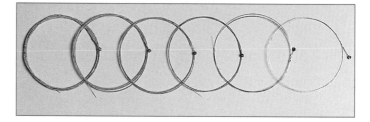

Strings vary in thickness from the bottom (thickest) to the top (thinnest). The bottom three are wound to give the sound more depth; the top three are just unwound alloy wire. When it's time to change your strings always check you have the right gauges.

The diameter of a string – its gauge – is measured in inches or centimetres: the lower the number, the thinner the string. A set of light gauge strings (0.09-0.42) may be preferable for electric guitar because it makes string-bending easier. A classical or Spanish guitar is intended to have nylon strings, in contrast to its steel-strung relative the folk acoustic guitar. If in doubt, consult your local music shop.

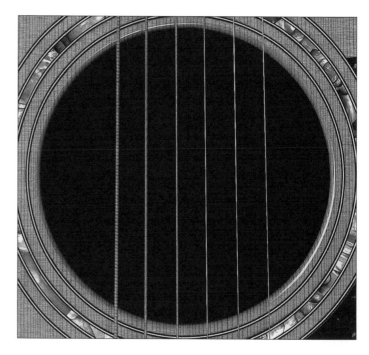

Following some simple guidelines will ensure that you always feel comfortable when playing.

1 Your arms should never take the weight of the guitar; they should be free just to play it.

2 Always keep the neck pointing slightly above the horizontal. Never let it point down toward the ground.

3 When practicing, it's more comfortable to sit down. Some players cross their legs right over left and rest the guitar on the right thigh, which elevates the instrument slightly.

Tip

Classical players have a seating posture of their own, using a footstool to raise the left foot, with the guitar tucked between the legs.

4 If you stand, you should not be supporting the guitar. Adjust the strap so the guitar is at a sensible height and position it so there is an equal balance of weight. When you take your hands away it should sit comfortably.

The electric guitarist

If you have an electric guitar, you'll also need an amplifier and a guitar lead to get a sound out of your instrument. Here's a step-by-step guide to setting up:

1 Attach your guitar strap. Make sure that the strap is adjusted to a comfortable length. A low-slung guitar looks really cool but is actually much more difficult to play – as long as your right and left hands feel comfortable on the guitar your position is probably right.

2 Plug one end of your guitar lead into the guitar. On a Les Paul type guitar (as shown here) the socket is on the underside of the body of the guitar. On a Fender Stratocaster type you will find the socket on the front of the guitar under the tone controls.

3 Take the other end of the lead and plug it into the socket marked input on your amplifier.

4 Adjust the volume controls on the amplifier and on your guitar until you can hear a sound from the amplifier.

If you can't hear any sound, check that the amp is plugged in and switched on, and that the volume control on your guitar is turned up.

Now you're ready to play!

If you're lucky enough to have an effects unit such as a distortion or wah-wah pedal you can have even more fun!

Effects pedals take the sound from your guitar and change it before it gets passed on to the amplifier. They can be powered by batteries or by a separate mains adaptor.

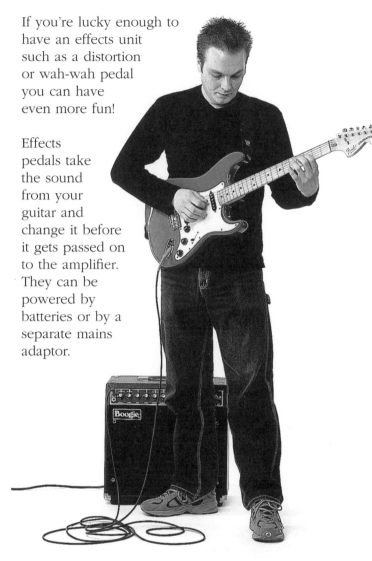

Take the other end of the lead that is plugged into your guitar and insert it into the input socket on the pedal (sometimes marked instrument).

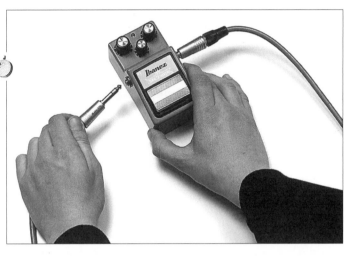

Then take another lead; insert one end of it into the pedal socket marked output (or amplifier) and the other end into the input socket on your amplifier.

The pedal is activated by simply stomping on the foot-operated switch. When the pedal is not switched on you should still be able hear the sound of your guitar as before - when you step on the switch the sound should change as the effect kicks in.

AWah-wah pedal produces a classic effect that you'll recognise instantly. You can plug it in in the same way as other effects pedals, and then vary the tone of your guitar sound by rocking back and forth on the pedal.

Once you're happy with your guitar set-up, turn up the volume and make some noise!

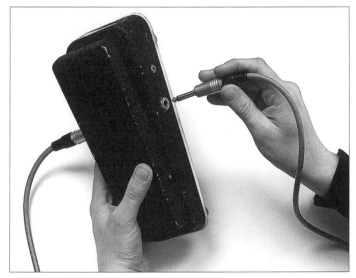

Right hand position

Your right hand can strum chords or pick single notes or you could use a pick (plectrum). The best way to start is to strum the strings. Either use a soft (bendy) pick or hold your thumb and first finger together as though you had an imaginary pick. Rest your forearm on the guitar so it can swing freely. Get used to the feel of your strumming hand against the strings.

Tip

Those of you who are left-handed, please swap the instructions around.

As an exercise, just strum the strings downwards from the 6th (lowest in pitch) to the 1st.

Then strum down again but go from the 4th to the 1st, missing out the 5th and 6th.

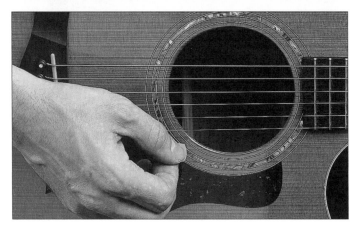

Once you're happy with the strumming motion, you can try finger-picking individual strings. The right hand adopts the following position:

1 Rest your forearm lightly on the guitar.

2 Arch your wrist so your fingers are approximately at 60 degrees to the back of your hand, then relax them so they become slightly curved.

Your right hand technique might depend on the sort of music you want to play. Folk and country players tend to strum (without a pick) or finger-pick, whereas rock guitarists use a pick for maximum volume! However, some rock guitarists, like Mark Knopfler, prefer to use their fingers to create a distinctive sound.

3 Place your thumb (p) on the 6th string, your index finger (i) on the 3rd string, your middle finger (m) on the 2nd string and your ring finger (a) on the 1st string. Try to make sure that your thumb comes in contact with the strings about an inch or so in front of your index finger.

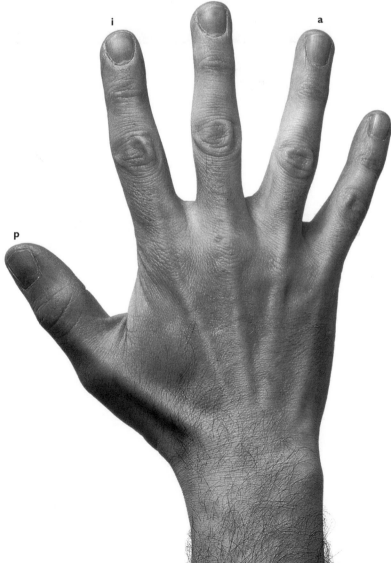

Holding the pick

The pick is held between the thumb and index finger of your strumming hand, which should be (roughly) at right angles to each other. Try out a few sizes and thicknesses of pick to find one you're comfortable with. Hold the pick securely and don't have too much of it protruding from your fingers toward the strings.

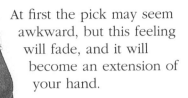

At first the pick may seem awkward, but this feeling will fade, and it will become an extension of your hand.

Play the open strings one at a time from the 6th to the 1st, then from the 5th to the 1st, 4th to the 1st and so on. Your pick should be hitting the upper side of each string and travelling toward the floor. This is known as a downstroke.

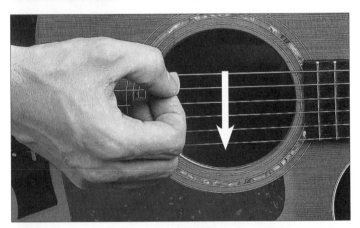

Now try strumming across the open strings with the pick – don't worry about your left hand at this stage, just get used to the sensation of the pick travelling across the strings.

Tip

Playing live can be a nerve-wracking experience – it's very easy to drop your plectrum in the heat and sweat of a rock gig. Pro players stick spare picks to the back of their guitar, or wedge them under the scratch-plate in case of emergencies!

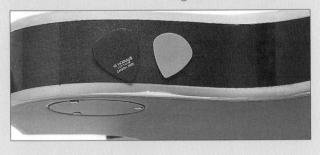

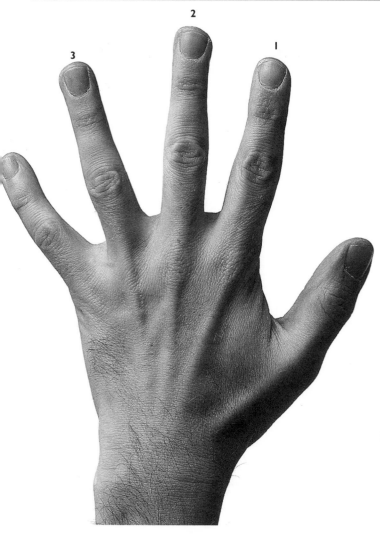

The first time you try a new chord you may find it hard to get the positioning of your fingers right, let alone press them down. If necessary, use your other hand to physically put each fretting finger in position.

The fretting fingers are numbered 1, 2, 3 and 4.

Try to keep the left hand relaxed. The left hand thumb should be roughly vertical behind the neck and roughly behind the 1st and 2nd fingers.

Once you feel confident holding your guitar, experiment with different playing positions to see what feels the most comfortable. Almost every conceivable playing position has been used at some point – although some are more difficult than others!

Tip

The first few weeks will be tough on your fingers. But don't worry! Gradually you'll develop pads of harder skin on the ends of each finger. You'll need to keep practicing to make sure they don't disappear!

CHECKPOINT

WHAT YOU'VE ACHIEVED SO FAR...

You can now:
• Hold your guitar comfortably
• Name each part of the guitar
• Strum with fingers or with a pick
• Choose appropriate strings for your guitar

Tuning your guitar

There are various ways of tuning the guitar – use the one that suits you best.

Using another instrument to tune to
The simplest way to make sure that your guitar is in tune is to find someone else with a tuned guitar and match each string on your guitar with the relevant string on the tuned guitar.

Alternatively, you could tune to a piano or electronic keyboard.

Refer to the diagram below to tune each string.

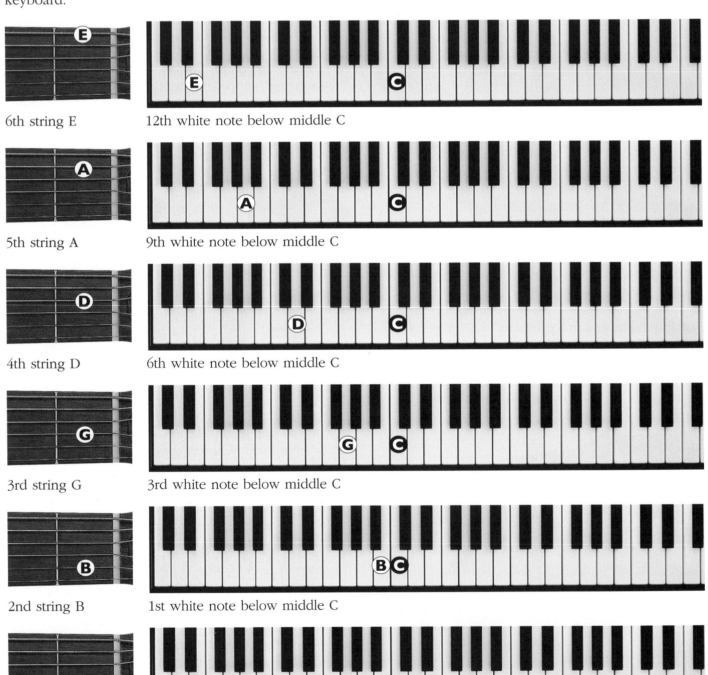

6th string E   12th white note below middle C

5th string A   9th white note below middle C

4th string D   6th white note below middle C

3rd string G   3rd white note below middle C

2nd string B   1st white note below middle C

1st string E   2nd white note above middle C

Tip

If you're not sure whether a note is sharp or flat
(i.e. too high or too low), loosen the string being tuned
a little and slowly bring it up to the required pitch.

This is perhaps the commonest method and one that works if you are pretty confident that at least one of the strings is in tune. Let's assume the bottom string (6th) is in tune. Being the thickest, you'll find that the 6th string probably won't drift out of tune as much as some of the others.

Follow the tuning diagram and tune from the bottom string upwards.

To tune:

6th to 5th string   5th to 4th string   4th to 3rd string   3rd to 2nd string   2nd to 1st string

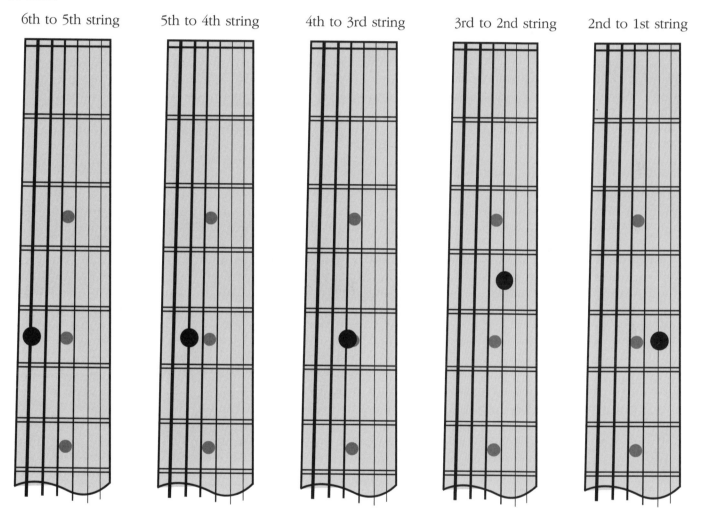

Track 1 of the CD gives tuning notes for each string, beginning with the 6th (lowest).

CHECKPOINT

WHAT YOU'VE ACHIEVED SO FAR...

You can now:
• Tune your guitar to a keyboard
• Use relative tuning
• Ensure that you are in tune with other musicians

Your first chord A

Now you've tuned up, let's play some chords. Besides learning the chord fingering, we're going to look at some simple strumming and work all the ideas into a song for you to play along with.

Compare how A looks in the photo to the chord box:

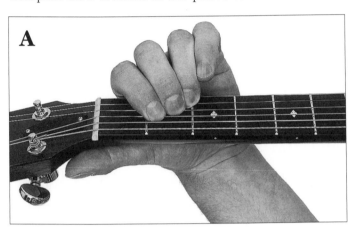

1 The fingers are placed just behind the 2nd fret. You never press down a string with a finger actually on the metal fret.

2 The fingers are angled to fit comfortably alongside each other and to fit in the narrow space.

3 The 6th string is not played; the 5th and 1st strings are 'open' (i.e. not fretted and shown as 0 in the chord box).

4 Keep the little finger out of the way so it doesn't catch the 1st string.

Now strum the whole chord – just downward strums at first.

 Track 2 demonstrates how the A chord should sound.

Chords for the guitar are pictured in the form of a 'chord box', where the six strings are viewed as though you're looking at the guitar neck face on with the strings going down the page. The numbers in circles tell you which fingers to use.

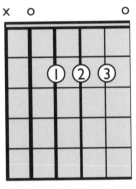

X = don't play this string
O = open string

Tip

If you're left-handed these numbers will stay the same, but the chord shape itself will be reversed.

Don't hit the bottom string!

A major facts:

1 The A chord's full name is A major – later on you'll come across other types of A chord such as minor and seventh.

2 The A chord is named after its lowest note – the open A string (the 5th string).

3 Like all major chords, A major is characterised by a bright, happy sound.

The number in the circle tells you which left hand finger to use.

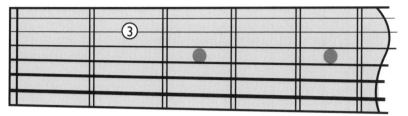

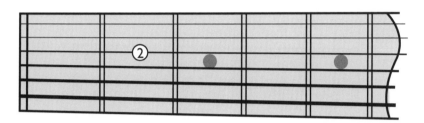

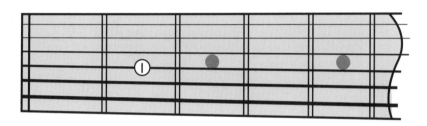

Final chord shape

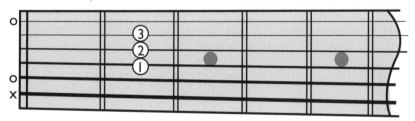

X = don't play this string   **O** = open string

Tip

Make sure you can hear all the notes clearly.
First play each string separately. If there is a buzz then something is wrong with the way you're holding down the note, or one of your other fingers is touching the adjacent string and preventing it ringing as it should. You may have to press harder to get rid of the buzz, or, if you can, move your finger slightly closer to the fret. Experiment until you can hear all the strings in the chord sounding.

The chord of D

Let's try the D chord next. It only has four notes, so don't play the E and A (6th and 5th) strings.

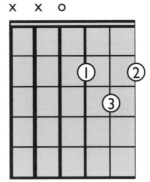

x x o

D

1 The 1st and 2nd fingers must avoid touching the B string (2nd string) for all the strings to sound clearly.

2 Keep your little finger out of the way as it can clutter the hand position.

3 Play the strings separately from bottom to top (4th to 1st) and make sure they are all sounding clearly.

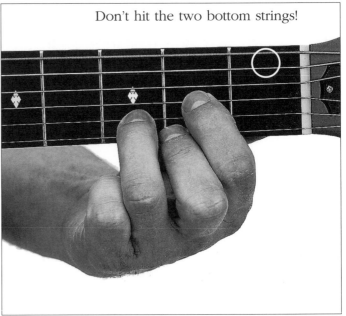

Don't hit the two bottom strings!

You have now learnt two of the most common chords in pop – A and D. These two chords sound great when played one after the other – you'll find this chord change in hundreds of classic songs.

4 Now strum the whole chord.

Listen to **Track 3** to hear how the chord should sound.

D major facts:

1 The D chord is named after its lowest note – the open D string (the 4th string).

2 D is a favourite with folk guitarists – try adding your fourth finger at the third fret on the top string to form a chord of Dsus4, for a classic folky sound.

3 D and A sound great when played after each other.

The number in the circle tells you which left hand finger to use.

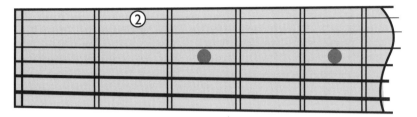

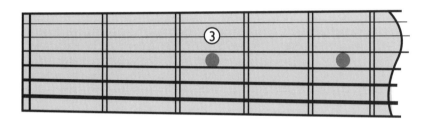

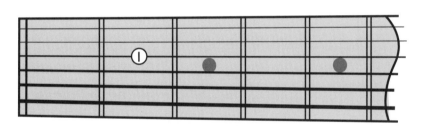

Final chord shape

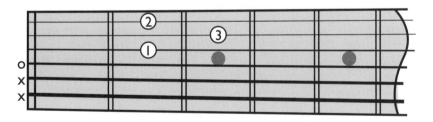

X = don't play this string   **O** = open string

Don't press down too hard with the fingers of your left hand – you'll be surprised how little pressure it actually takes to fret a chord successfully. Positioning your thumb comfortably behind the neck can be helpful.

The chord of E

This chord has inspired many classic riffs and songs, and sounds great because you can play all six strings. There are just three strings to fret (5th, 4th and 3rd):

E

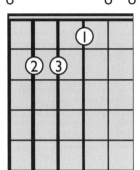

E is a powerful-sounding chord as all six strings are played, including the open E strings which ring out.

Listen to **Track 4** to hear how it should sound.

1 Although the E chord is a relatively simple shape, be careful not to catch your 3rd finger on the 3rd string – this will stop the note ringing. Your end finger joints should adopt more of a vertical position above the string to avoid this.

2 Relax the thumb and arch the wrist for the best position.

E major facts:

1 The E chord is the fullest sounding of all the chords you've learnt so far – because, unlike A or D, it uses all six strings.

2 E is possibly the most popular key for guitar music, because it allows you to use the open E strings (top and bottom strings).

3 Once you've perfected the E shape, try adding your little finger at the 2nd fret, 3rd string, to form the chord of Esus4.

▼ **The Jimi Hendrix classic 'Hey Joe' relies heavily on the chord of E**

The number in the circle tells you which left hand finger to use.

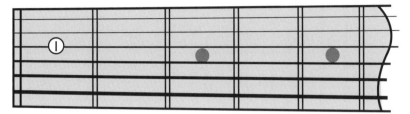

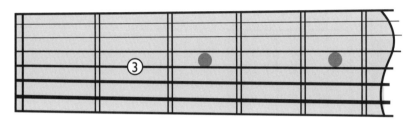

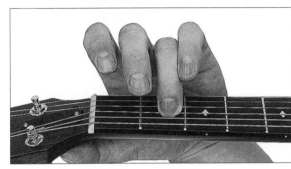

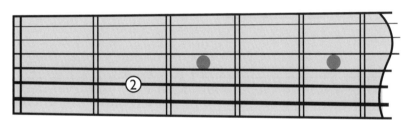

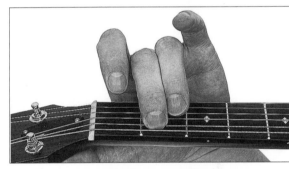

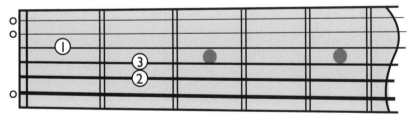

Final chord shape

X = don't play this string   **O** = open string

A, D & E – the three-chord trick

The chords of A, D & E can be played in almost any sequence and they will sound good.

In fact, lots of classic rock songs can be played using only these three chords – check out 'Wild Thing', 'Peggy Sue', or just about any blues tune to hear the three-chord trick in action.

CHECKPOINT
WHAT YOU'VE ACHIEVED SO FAR...

You can now:
• Play the chords of A, D and E major
• Strum 4, 5 or 6 string chords

Let's play!

Now that you're familiar with the chord shapes of A, D and E, let's do some playing!

In rhythm with A
Let's return to the chord of A. It doesn't matter whether you use a pick or not – but can you strum downward from the 5th string to the 1st without any buzzes?

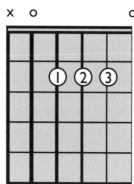

Using The Audio

There are two tracks on the CD for each example given here. The first is a full version with guitar, the second has the same backing but without the guitar part, so that you can play along. You'll soon get used to strumming in time with the music and eventually you'll be able to perform a smooth chord change with no problems.

Treble Clef

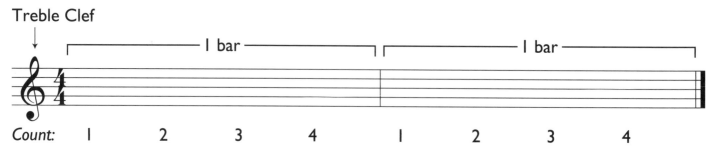

Count: 1   2   3   4   1   2   3   4

Don't worry about the musical notation at this stage – later we'll use a very simple system to indicate rhythm but for now all you need to concentrate on is counting four beats per bar, as indicated below the staff (or stave).

The next example (see page 25) will get you started, with the chord of A!

Tip

The ⌐ means that you should strum each chord with a "downstroke" – moving from the strings nearest the top of the guitar downwards towards the ground.

Track 5 starts with four clicks to give you the tempo. The track is just one bar repeated over and over, with the first beat accented, or played louder, so you can spot the start of each bar. Strum the A chord on the first beat of the bar.

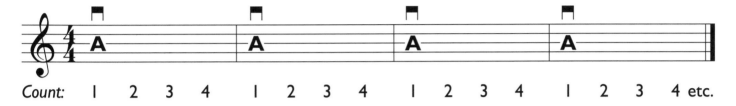

Count: 1   2   3   4   1   2   3   4   1   2   3   4   1   2   3   4 etc.

⊓ = downstroke

Sometimes it helps to count aloud while playing – alternatively you can tap your foot on the beat.

Track 6 gives you a chance to play along with the band.

Now let's play the same A chord twice a bar instead of once. Count four beats in a bar, and then strum the A chord as you count "one" and "three".

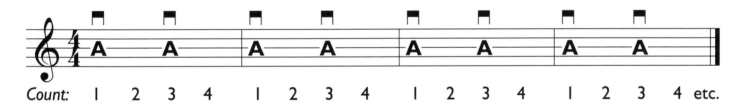

Count: 1   2   3   4   1   2   3   4   1   2   3   4   1   2   3   4 etc.

Track 7 demonstrates how this should sound.

Track 8 is your chance to go solo!

And now let's strum the A chord on each beat – use a downstroke as you count the four beats in each bar.

Count: 1   2   3   4   1   2   3   4   1   2   3   4   1   2   3   4 etc.

Track 9 demonstrates strumming on each beat and

Track 10 gives you the track minus the recorded guitar part, this time with no accents. Accent the first beat of each bar as you strum.

Upstroke/downstroke

The final strumming pattern requires you to strum up as well as down. Practice strumming as before with downstrokes, and then gradually try to catch the strings as you raise your hand back up again to strum downwards.

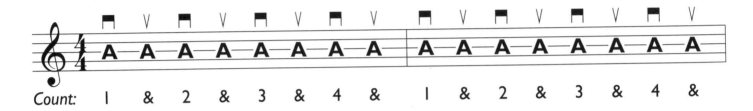

Count: 1 & 2 & 3 & 4 &   1 & 2 & 3 & 4 &

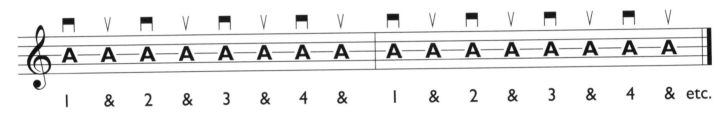

1 & 2 & 3 & 4 &   1 & 2 & 3 & 4 & etc.

◼ = downstroke

V = upstroke

These upstrokes occur between the beats: count **1** & **2** & **3** & **4** & throughout the bar – downstrokes should fall on the numbers, and upstrokes should fall on the "&"s.

When you hear **Track 11**, it will be obvious what's happening. However, continue to count the main beats as you strum and accent the first beat of each bar.

Track 12 is the backing track with only the first beat accented. Listen to the hi-hat in the drum part – that's the rhythm that you need to follow – and then try playing along.

Speed up your learning

1 Try to find time to practice every day – even if it's only for 10 minutes. It's much better to practice every day for 10 minutes than it is to practice once a week for two hours!

2 Identify chord shapes and techniques that you find difficult and practice them slowly and deliberately.

3 Pick each string of the chord and make sure that it is ringing out clearly before you start strumming.

In rhythm with D

Now that you are familiar with the A chord, let's also practice strumming the D and E chords you have learnt.

D

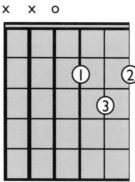

Listen to **Track 13** (with four clicks intro) and then strum once a bar on beat 1 along with **Track 14**.

D	D	D	D
1 2 3 4	1 2 3 4	1 2 3 4	1 2 3 4 etc.

Track 15 demonstrates two strums of D on beats 1 and 3.

Play along with **Track 16**.

D D	D D	D D	D D
1 2 3 4	1 2 3 4	1 2 3 4	1 2 3 4 etc.

Now play four D chords in each bar, using a downstroke on each beat.

Listen to **Track 17** to hear how it should sound,

and then try over the backing track, **Track 18**.

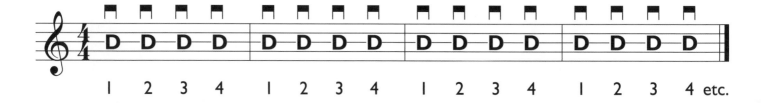

D D D D	D D D D	D D D D	D D D D
1 2 3 4	1 2 3 4	1 2 3 4	1 2 3 4 etc.

Track 19 uses downstrokes and upstrokes in continuous rhythm.

Track 20 is the backing track with the first beat of each bar accented.

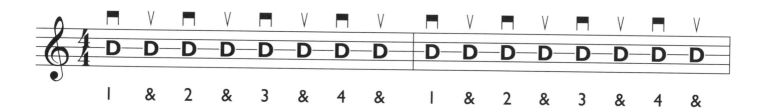

D D D D D D D D | D D D D D D D D

1 & 2 & 3 & 4 & 1 & 2 & 3 & 4 &

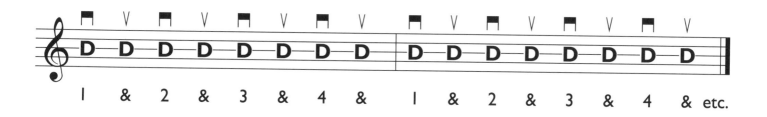

D D D D D D D D | D D D D D D D D

1 & 2 & 3 & 4 & 1 & 2 & 3 & 4 & etc.

Remember you only need to strum the top four strings to make the chord of D – the bottom two strings should be avoided.

In rhythm with E

Here are the same exercises on the E chord.

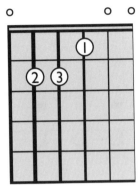

Track 21 demonstrates one strum of E per bar (remember the four clicks of the intro).

Track 22 is the backing track with an accent on beat 1.

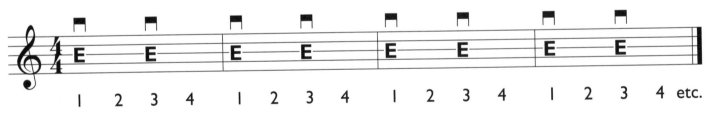

Track 23 has two strums per bar on beats 1 and 3.

Track 24 is the backing track with accents on beats 1 and 3.

Track 25 requires four strums of E, one per beat of the bar, all downstrokes.

Track 26 is the backing track with accents on beat 1.

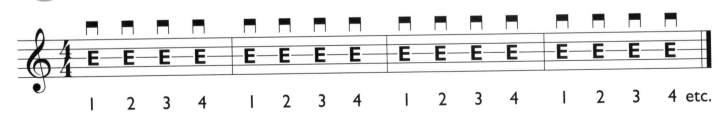

Track 27 uses downstrokes and upstrokes in continuous rhythm.

Track 28 is the backing track with the first beat of each bar accented.

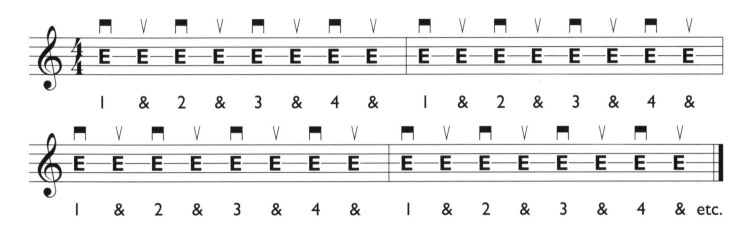

1 & 2 & 3 & 4 & 1 & 2 & 3 & 4 &

1 & 2 & 3 & 4 & 1 & 2 & 3 & 4 & etc.

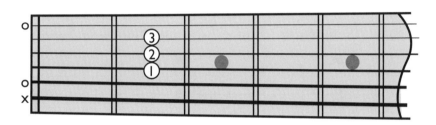

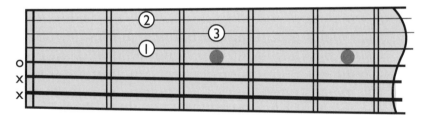

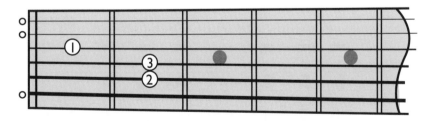

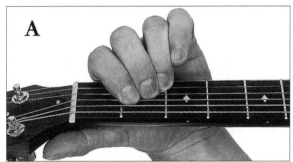

A

D

E

CHECKPOINT

WHAT YOU'VE ACHIEVED SO FAR...

You can now:

• Strum 3 major chords in time with backing tracks using upstrokes and downstrokes

• Follow a basic musical score

Moving around!

Now it's time to try changing chords from bar to bar.

For **Track 29** let's use only downstrokes and play one chord per bar.

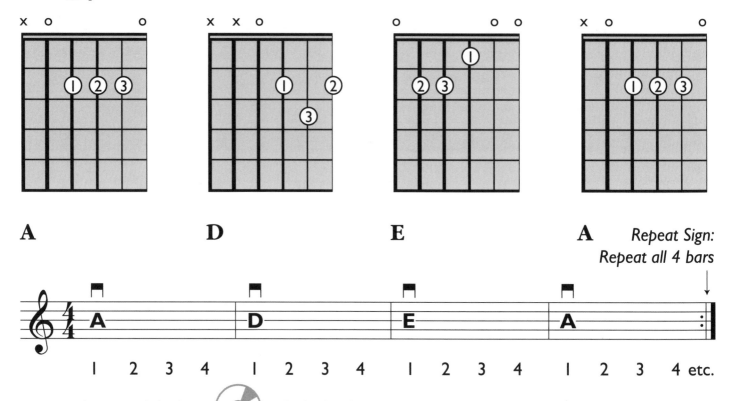

A   **D**   **E**   **A**   *Repeat Sign: Repeat all 4 bars*

| A | D | E | A |

| 1 2 3 4 | 1 2 3 4 | 1 2 3 4 | 1 2 3 4 etc. |

Now try playing with backing **Track 30**. Think ahead and prepare the next shape chord as soon as you've played the previous one.

Now try two strums per chord – i.e. on beats 1 and 2 of each bar. This leaves you the duration of beats 3 and 4 to change to the next shape. Can you feel when to change chord?

Once you've perfected two strums per bar, try moving up to three chords per bar (on beats 1, 2 and 3). This only gives you one beat to change between chord shapes!

Listen to **Track 31** to hear how this should sound,

and then try yourself over the backing **Track 32**.

repeat

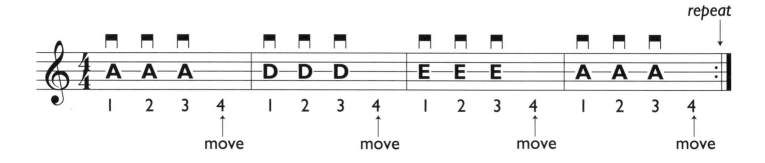

| A A A | D D D | E E E | A A A |

| 1 2 3 4 | 1 2 3 4 | 1 2 3 4 | 1 2 3 4 |
| move | move | move | move |

Tip

If you can't change chord fast enough initially, just ignore the strumming and simply move from one chord to the next in your own time until it feels comfortable.

The next step is to play the upstrokes as well.

First, strum beats 1 and 2 with down and up strokes and change chord shapes during beats 3 and 4.

Then, with **Track 32**, strum beats 1, 2 and 3 and change during beat 4.

Finally, try strumming up and down on beats 1, 2, 3 and 4, changing chord shape quickly before the start of the next bar.

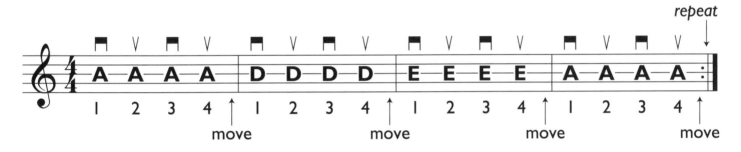

The objective is to make the chord changes as quick and smooth as possible. Try to strum for longer and longer, leaving less and less time for your left hand to change shape.

Listen to **Track 33** to hear how this should sound.

Eventually, you will be strumming 8 times a bar (4 up and 4 down) and you'll have to change shape in between the last upstroke of one bar and the first downstroke of the next one.

Track 34 is the backing track. A crash cymbal indicates the beginning of the four bar pattern.

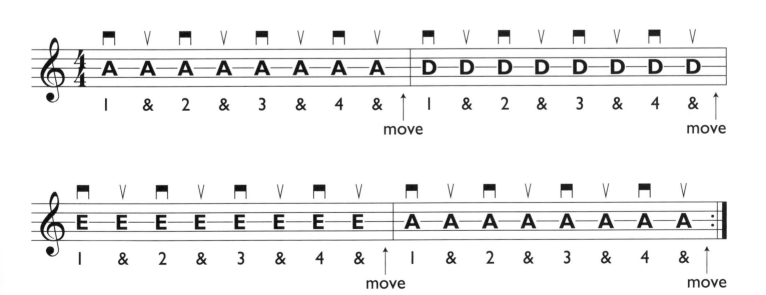

The chord of G

To play the song that follows you need two extra chords, G and C.

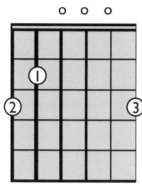

Notice how the 1st and 2nd fingers arch over to come down on the strings so as to avoid catching the open strings.

To hear how it should sound, check out **Track 35**.

To practice G, try these exercises. First, strum the G chord on the first beat of the bar only.

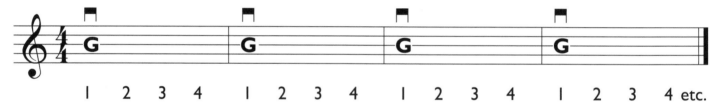

Listen to **Track 36** to hear how this sounds.

Track 37 is the backing track with only the first beat of each accented.

The next pattern uses up and down strumming – count steadily and try and keep your strumming arm relaxed as you play.

Tip

Use the same strum patterns as you have been practicing to get used to strumming the new chord of G.

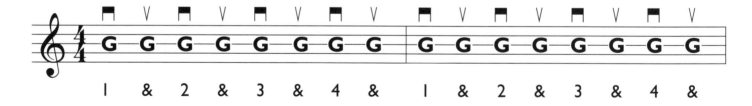

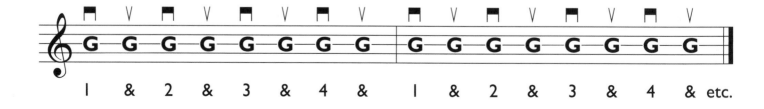

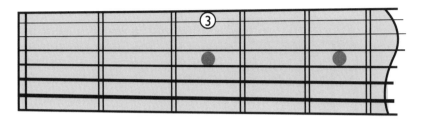

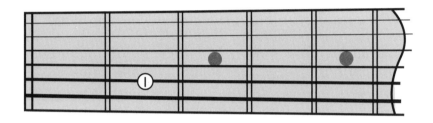

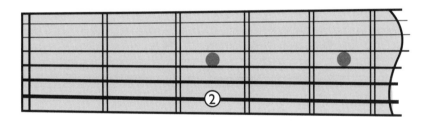

Final chord shape

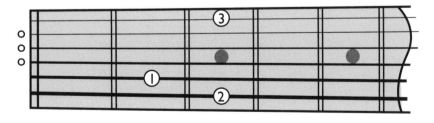

O = open string

Once again, care must be taken not to muffle the open fourth and second strings with the fretting fingers.

The chord of C

This chord is slightly more difficult than the four you have already learnt, because an open string is hidden in the middle of the chord shape.

C

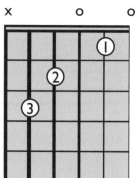

The first finger has to be almost vertical to clear the 1st string, so make sure your nails are short enough to press down onto the 2nd string in this way. Watch out that you don't catch your 2nd finger against the open 3rd string (G).

Track 38 demonstrates how it sounds – make sure you don't strike the bottom string!

Now strum the chord against the rhythm track, one strum per bar.

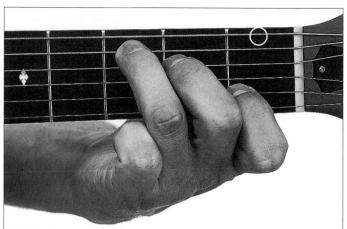

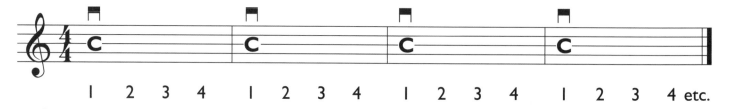

Track 39 demonstrates how this example should sound.

Track 40 is your chance to practice your strumming technique.

Now try strumming up and down strokes, accenting the first beat each time.

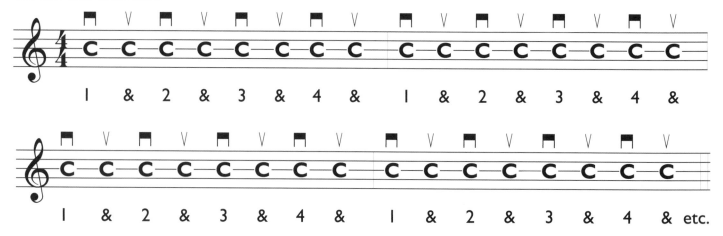

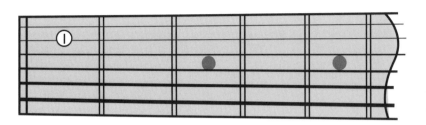

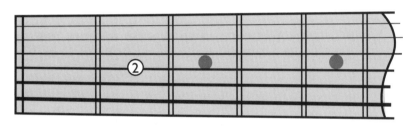

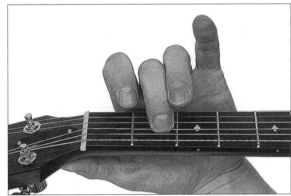

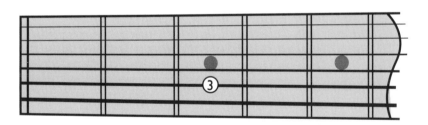

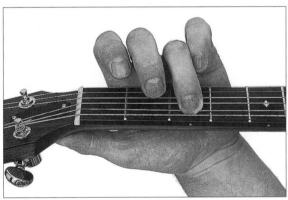

Final chord shape

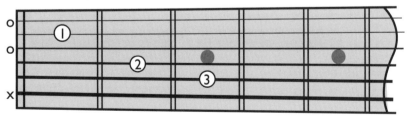

X = don't play this string   **O** = open string

Be careful not to catch the open third string with your second finger, and similarly, don't muffle the open top string with your first finger.

Once again, if you attempt to make your fingers meet the fingerboard at right angles you shouldn't have any problems.

Your first song

Now let's take all five chords and play a complete song!

A

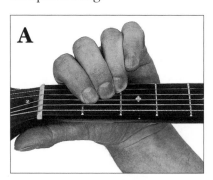

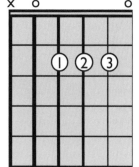

D

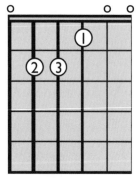

E

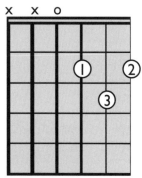

G

C

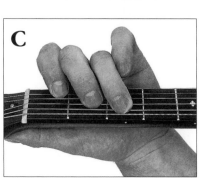

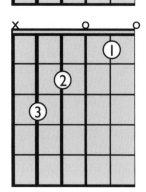

Listen to **Track 41** and follow the musical example opposite until you are familiar with all the chord sequences in the song.

Understanding Musical Notation
Don't be put off by the musical signs we've used here – this is how it works:

1 Play through the Intro in exactly the same way as you have played all the other examples in this book – count steadily and play the chords as indicated.

2 Carry on through the **Solo/melody** until you come to the :‖ sign – that's a repeat sign, and it means you have to go back to A and play that section again.

3 The second time through miss out the bars under the number 1 and go straight to the bars under the number 2.

4 Ignore the **To Coda ⊕** sign for the time being and carry straight on into the next section – there's another repeat here.

5 Once you've repeated that sequence carry on until you reach the marking **D. 𝄋. al Coda** – this basically means "Go back to the 𝄋 until you reach the **To Coda ⊕** marking, and then go to the **Coda**.

6 So skip back to letter A and play through that repeated section again until you reach the **To Coda ⊕** marking.

7 Then go to **⊕ Coda** and play through that section until the end.

Now try playing along with **Track 43**.

Tip
I Make sure all the chords sound cleanly – no buzzes!
2 Play in time, with the chords on the beat. Don't worry about playing a continuous rhythm right away. Just get comfortable with the changes, and introduce more strumming as you gain confidence.

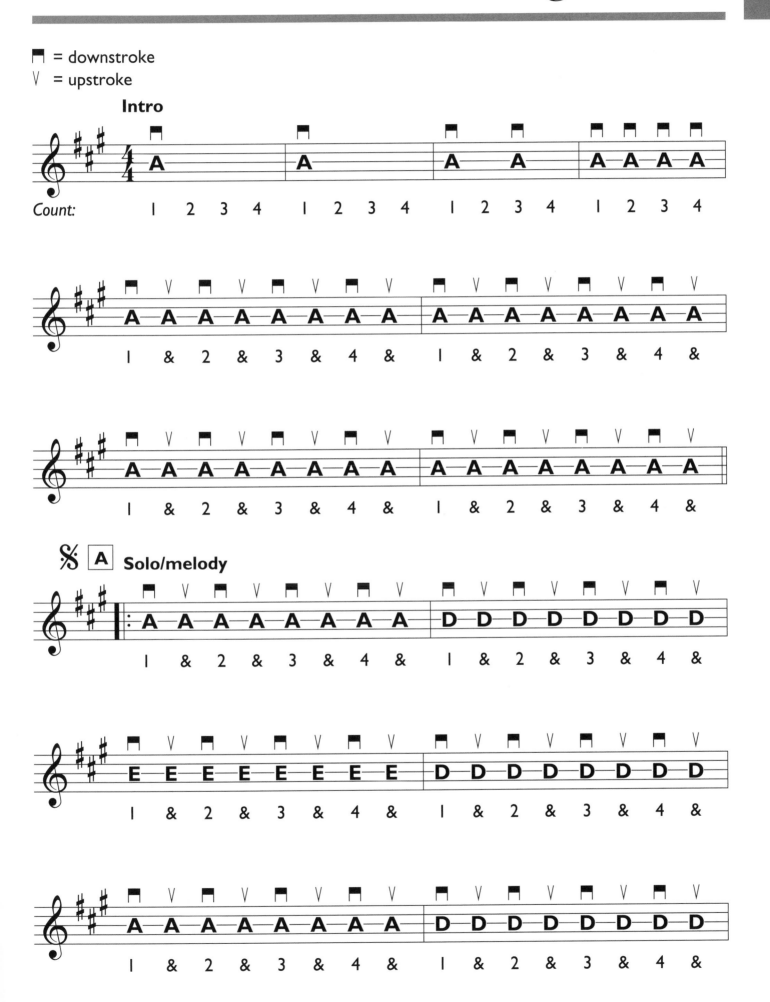

Changin' Time

1st & 2nd endings: play through the bars under the '1', then skip back to A
On the second pass, leave out the bars under '1', and go directly to the bars under '2'.

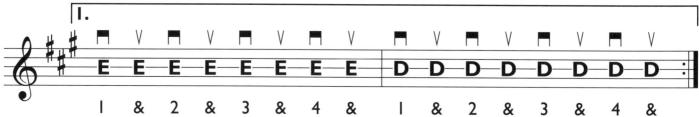

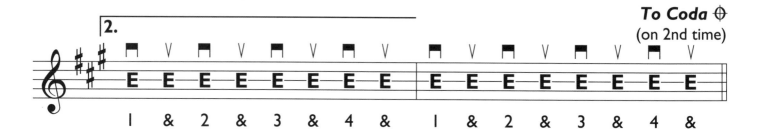

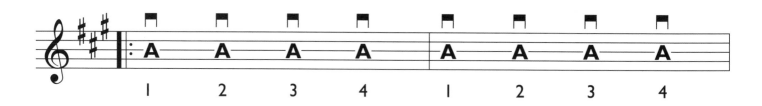

Skip back to the Sign (%) at **A** and play through the 1st & 2nd endings.
Then, at To Coda ⊕ , skip ahead to the Coda below to finish the song.

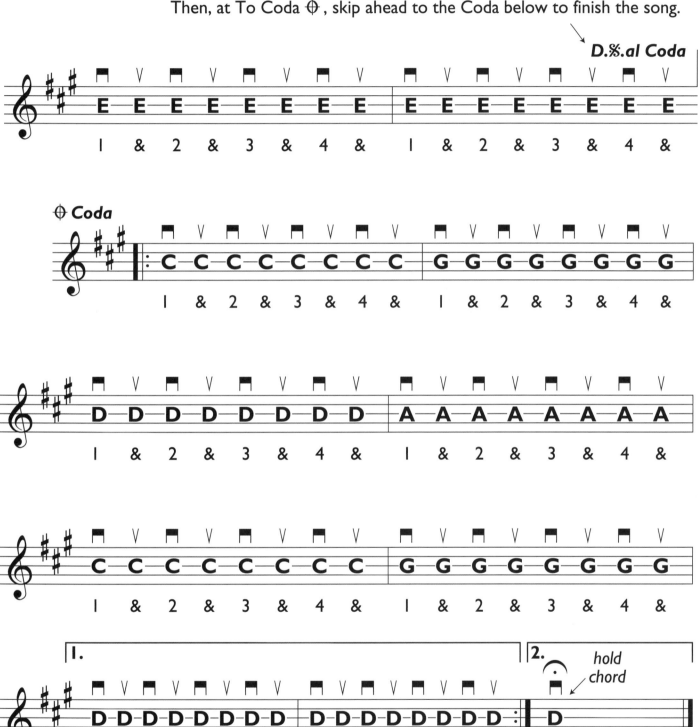

Some other chords

Here are some other essential chord shapes:

Remember that not all chords use all six strings – so take care which strings you hit!

A minor

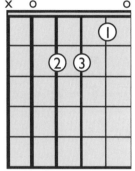

Don't strike the 6th string!

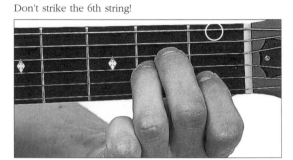

E minor

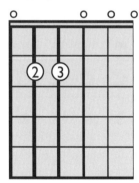

D7

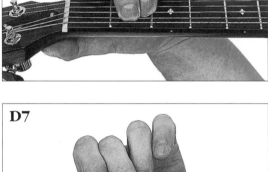

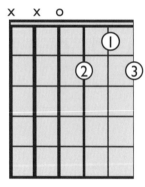

Don't strike the 5th and 6th strings!

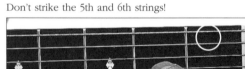

E7

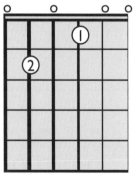

Don't strike the 6th string!

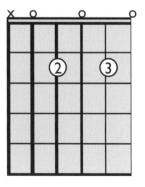

A7

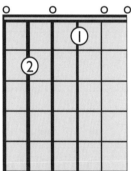

Now that you're comfortable with the world of chords let's finish with a simple guitar melody that you can play along with the song you've just learned.

Introduction to TAB

Most guitar music uses a system called "tablature" (TAB) which tells you where to put your fingers when playing the single notes of a melody.

To play the simple melody of the song let's briefly look at the TAB system.

1 Don't concern yourself with the music notation for now, concentrate on the TAB information. TAB is always written under the melody of the song.

2 The six horizontal lines of the TAB represent the six strings of your guitar; the bottom line represents the lowest (thickest) string, and the top line represents the highest (thinnest) string.

3 The number on those horizontal lines indicate the fret at which you should place your finger.

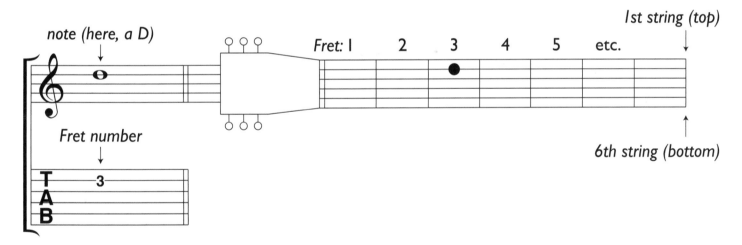

In the above example, the note is a D and is found at the 3rd fret of the 2nd string. You place your left hand finger just behind the 3rd fret on the 2nd string.

Tip

Open strings are designated as 0 on the TAB line – don't fret the string, just play it open.

Adding a melody

Now you're ready to add the melody to "Changin' Time". Listen to **Track 42** to hear how this sounds. Practice it really slowly at first, concentrating on counting steadily. Once you're confident of the sequence of notes, build up the speed gradually until you can play along with **Track 43**.

There's no melody in the Intro so you'll have to count really carefully in order to come in in the right place. Listen to **Track 42** again until you're completely familiar with the song- then you'll be able to feel when it's the right time to start playing the melody.

After you've repeated the Solo/Melody section, there's no melody until you reach the "D.S. al Coda" instruction, which then returns you to letter [A].

Finally, there's a slightly modified form of the tune in the Coda, which will take you through to the end of the song.

Counting

Counting is one vital skill that all musicians need to master – especially if you ever want to play in a band.

In this song there are substantial gaps when there's no melody to play – carry on counting 4 beats in a bar, but use the first beat of each bar as a count of how many bars you've rested for, e.g.

1 2 3 4, **2** 2 3 4, **3** 2 3 4, **4** 2 3 4 etc

Then you'll be ready for the moment when you have to start playing again.

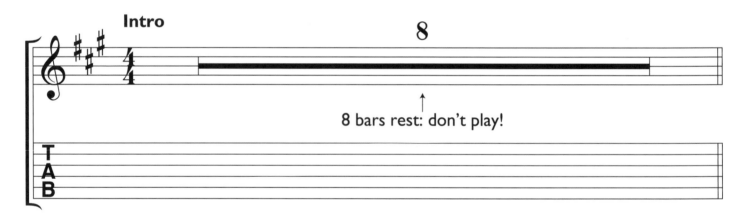

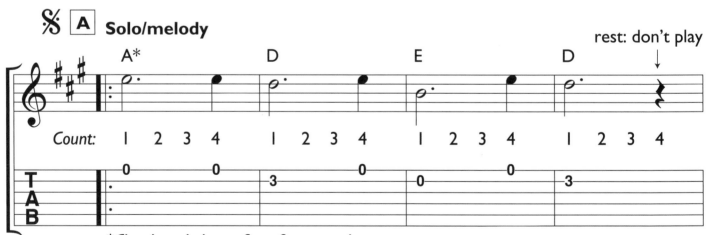

Chord symbols are for reference only.

Congratulations!

I hope that you have enjoyed playing through this book and that you will feel inspired to continue making music on your guitar in whichever style most interests you. Feel free to ask other players about their experience and techniques – they'll be able to pass on some useful tips and advice.

If you've made it this far, you've learned five of the most important guitar chords, and, more importantly, you have learned to change between them smoothly.

You've learnt to strum in various patterns, using both up and downstrokes and you've developed your sense of rhythm so that you can play along with backing tracks.

Finally, you've put all those skills together and learned a complete song, with a solo guitar melody.

Armed with the skills you've learned in this book, you're now ready to tackle some classic songs. Check out some of the tunes listed below, and listen carefully to the guitar parts – most of them are simple chord changes using the chords introduced in this book.

Don't Look Back In Anger Oasis
Everybody Hurts R.E.M.
Everything Must Go Manic Street Preachers

Hey Joe Jimi Hendrix
How Soon Is Now? The Smiths
Jumping Jack Flash The Rolling Stones
Parklife Blur
Smells Like Teen Spirit Nirvana
Tears In Heaven Eric Clapton
Waterfall The Stone Roses
Wild Thing The Troggs
Won't Get Fooled Again The Who
Yesterday The Beatles

Eric Clapton

Keith Richard
The Rolling Stones

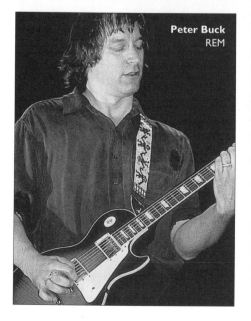

Peter Buck
REM

Kurt Cobain
Nirvana

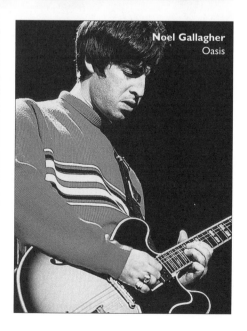

Noel Gallagher
Oasis

TEACH YOURSELF GUITAR

Learn how to play notes, chords, and chord progressions while using the book and accompanying audio tracks. Covers everything from holding the guitar and tuning, to chord study and fingerpicking. Topics also cover the use of picks as well as guitar tablature. Perfect for the beginner to learn songs right away on the guitar.

TABLATURE

Book and DVD, 32 pages
ISBN 0.8256.1890.8
UPC 7.52187.97131.3
AM971311

TEACH YOURSELF HARMONICA

Your all-in-one package to learning to play the harmonica. Learn how to care for your instrument, play chords, and practice tonguing. Then advance to playing both single note and chord-melody songs, bending notes, playing riffs, and practicing six different styles of harmonica songs. Beginners will be learning songs right away with this winning method.

Book and DVD, 32 pages
ISBN 0.8256.1892.6
UPC 7.52187.97133.7
AM971333

TEACH YOURSELF KEYBOARD

Designed for the learner to understand the keys and play scales and chords for any keyboard. Learn all the basics from proper hand positioning to music notation. Then move on to chords, arpeggios, rests and scales, all while using the methods learned to begin playing songs.

Book and DVD, 32 pages
ISBN 0.8256.1891.6
UPC 7.52187.97132.0
AM971322